THIS I
BELONGS TO.

CONTACT INFORMATION

NAME:

ADDRESS:

PHONE:

START / END DATES

TO

FIELD OBSERVATIONS

DATE:

TIME:

LOCATION / HABITAT:

SEASON:

WEATHER:

BIRD NAME:

BIRD NAME:

SCIENTIFIC NAME:

OF BIRDS SPOTTED: 1   2   3   4   5   6   7   8   9   10   11+

SIGHTS:

SOUNDS:

APPEARANCE:

OBSERVATIONS:

ACTIVITY:

FIELD OBSERVATIONS

IMPRESSIONS:

EQUIPMENT / FURNISHINGS:

RECOMMENDED GUIDE BOOK(S):

RECOMMENDED MAPS(S):

DRIVING/HIKING DIRECTIONS:

PHOTO

IMAGE FILE NAME:

CAMERA EQUIPMENT:

SKETCH

MARKINGS/FEATURES:

BIRD SIGHTINGS SPECIES	HABITAT	QUANTITY

BIRD SIGHTINGS SPECIES	HABITAT	QUANTITY

FIELD OBSERVATIONS

DATE:	TIME:

LOCATION / HABITAT:

SEASON:	WEATHER:

BIRD NAME:

BIRD NAME:

SCIENTIFIC NAME:

OF BIRDS SPOTTED: 1   2   3   4   5   6   7   8   9   10   11+

SIGHTS:

SOUNDS:

APPEARANCE:

OBSERVATIONS:

ACTIVITY:

FIELD OBSERVATIONS

IMPRESSIONS:

EQUIPMENT / FURNISHINGS:

RECOMMENDED GUIDE BOOK(S):

RECOMMENDED MAPS(S):

DRIVING/HIKING DIRECTIONS:

PHOTO

IMAGE FILE NAME:

CAMERA EQUIPMENT:

SKETCH

MARKINGS/FEATURES:

BIRD SIGHTINGS SPECIES	HABITAT	QUANTITY

BIRD SIGHTINGS SPECIES	HABITAT	QUANTITY

FIELD OBSERVATIONS

DATE:

TIME:

LOCATION / HABITAT:

SEASON:

WEATHER:

BIRD NAME:

BIRD NAME:

SCIENTIFIC NAME:

OF BIRDS SPOTTED: 1   2   3   4   5   6   7   8   9   10   11+

SIGHTS:

SOUNDS:

APPEARANCE:

OBSERVATIONS:

ACTIVITY:

FIELD OBSERVATIONS

IMPRESSIONS:

EQUIPMENT / FURNISHINGS:

RECOMMENDED GUIDE BOOK(S):

RECOMMENDED MAPS(S):

DRIVING/HIKING DIRECTIONS:

PHOTO

IMAGE FILE NAME:

CAMERA EQUIPMENT:

SKETCH

MARKINGS/FEATURES:

BIRD SIGHTINGS SPECIES	HABITAT	QUANTITY

BIRD SIGHTINGS SPECIES	HABITAT	QUANTITY

FIELD OBSERVATIONS

DATE:

TIME:

LOCATION / HABITAT:

SEASON:

WEATHER:

BIRD NAME:

BIRD NAME:

SCIENTIFIC NAME:

OF BIRDS SPOTTED: 1   2   3   4   5   6   7   8   9   10   11+

SIGHTS:

SOUNDS:

APPEARANCE:

OBSERVATIONS:

ACTIVITY:

FIELD OBSERVATIONS

IMPRESSIONS:

EQUIPMENT / FURNISHINGS:

RECOMMENDED GUIDE BOOK(S):

RECOMMENDED MAPS(S):

DRIVING/HIKING DIRECTIONS:

PHOTO

IMAGE FILE NAME:

CAMERA EQUIPMENT:

SKETCH

MARKINGS/FEATURES:

BIRD SIGHTINGS SPECIES	HABITAT	QUANTITY

BIRD SIGHTINGS SPECIES	HABITAT	QUANTITY

FIELD OBSERVATIONS

DATE: | TIME:

LOCATION / HABITAT:

SEASON: | WEATHER:

BIRD NAME:

BIRD NAME:

SCIENTIFIC NAME:

OF BIRDS SPOTTED: 1   2   3   4   5   6   7   8   9   10   11+

SIGHTS:

SOUNDS:

APPEARANCE:

OBSERVATIONS:

ACTIVITY:

FIELD OBSERVATIONS

IMPRESSIONS:

EQUIPMENT / FURNISHINGS:

RECOMMENDED GUIDE BOOK(S):

RECOMMENDED MAPS(S):

DRIVING/HIKING DIRECTIONS:

PHOTO

IMAGE FILE NAME:

CAMERA EQUIPMENT:

SKETCH

MARKINGS/FEATURES:

BIRD SIGHTINGS SPECIES	HABITAT	QUANTITY

BIRD SIGHTINGS SPECIES	HABITAT	QUANTITY

FIELD OBSERVATIONS

DATE:

TIME:

LOCATION / HABITAT:

SEASON:

WEATHER:

BIRD NAME:

BIRD NAME:

SCIENTIFIC NAME:

OF BIRDS SPOTTED: 1   2   3   4   5   6   7   8   9   10   11+

SIGHTS:

SOUNDS:

APPEARANCE:

OBSERVATIONS:

ACTIVITY:

FIELD OBSERVATIONS

IMPRESSIONS:

EQUIPMENT / FURNISHINGS:

RECOMMENDED GUIDE BOOK(S):

RECOMMENDED MAPS(S):

DRIVING/HIKING DIRECTIONS:

PHOTO

IMAGE FILE NAME:

CAMERA EQUIPMENT:

SKETCH

MARKINGS/FEATURES:

BIRD SIGHTINGS SPECIES	HABITAT	QUANTITY

BIRD SIGHTINGS SPECIES	HABITAT	QUANTITY

FIELD OBSERVATIONS

DATE:

TIME:

LOCATION / HABITAT:

SEASON:

WEATHER:

BIRD NAME:

BIRD NAME:

SCIENTIFIC NAME:

OF BIRDS SPOTTED: 1   2   3   4   5   6   7   8   9   10   11+

SIGHTS:

SOUNDS:

APPEARANCE:

OBSERVATIONS:

ACTIVITY:

FIELD OBSERVATIONS

IMPRESSIONS:

EQUIPMENT / FURNISHINGS:

RECOMMENDED GUIDE BOOK(S):

RECOMMENDED MAPS(S):

DRIVING/HIKING DIRECTIONS:

PHOTO

IMAGE FILE NAME:

CAMERA EQUIPMENT:

SKETCH

MARKINGS/FEATURES:

BIRD SIGHTINGS SPECIES	HABITAT	QUANTITY

BIRD SIGHTINGS SPECIES	HABITAT	QUANTITY

FIELD OBSERVATIONS

DATE:	TIME:

LOCATION / HABITAT:

SEASON:	WEATHER:

BIRD NAME:

BIRD NAME:

SCIENTIFIC NAME:

OF BIRDS SPOTTED: 1   2   3   4   5   6   7   8   9   10   11+

SIGHTS:

SOUNDS:

APPEARANCE:

OBSERVATIONS:

ACTIVITY:

FIELD OBSERVATIONS

IMPRESSIONS:

EQUIPMENT / FURNISHINGS:

RECOMMENDED GUIDE BOOK(S):

RECOMMENDED MAPS(S):

DRIVING/HIKING DIRECTIONS:

PHOTO

IMAGE FILE NAME:

CAMERA EQUIPMENT:

SKETCH

MARKINGS/FEATURES:

BIRD SIGHTINGS SPECIES	HABITAT	QUANTITY

BIRD SIGHTINGS SPECIES	HABITAT	QUANTITY

FIELD OBSERVATIONS

DATE:

TIME:

LOCATION / HABITAT:

SEASON:

WEATHER:

BIRD NAME:

BIRD NAME:

SCIENTIFIC NAME:

OF BIRDS SPOTTED: 1   2   3   4   5   6   7   8   9   10   11+

SIGHTS:

SOUNDS:

APPEARANCE:

OBSERVATIONS:

ACTIVITY:

FIELD OBSERVATIONS

IMPRESSIONS:

EQUIPMENT / FURNISHINGS:

RECOMMENDED GUIDE BOOK(S):

RECOMMENDED MAPS(S):

DRIVING/HIKING DIRECTIONS:

PHOTO

IMAGE FILE NAME:

CAMERA EQUIPMENT:

SKETCH

MARKINGS/FEATURES:

BIRD SIGHTINGS SPECIES	HABITAT	QUANTITY

BIRD SIGHTINGS SPECIES	HABITAT	QUANTITY

FIELD OBSERVATIONS

DATE:

TIME:

LOCATION / HABITAT:

SEASON:

WEATHER:

BIRD NAME:

BIRD NAME:

SCIENTIFIC NAME:

OF BIRDS SPOTTED: 1   2   3   4   5   6   7   8   9   10   11+

SIGHTS:

SOUNDS:

APPEARANCE:

OBSERVATIONS:

ACTIVITY:

FIELD OBSERVATIONS

IMPRESSIONS:

EQUIPMENT / FURNISHINGS:

RECOMMENDED GUIDE BOOK(S):

RECOMMENDED MAPS(S):

DRIVING/HIKING DIRECTIONS:

PHOTO

IMAGE FILE NAME:

CAMERA EQUIPMENT:

SKETCH

MARKINGS/FEATURES:

BIRD SIGHTINGS SPECIES	HABITAT	QUANTITY

BIRD SIGHTINGS SPECIES	HABITAT	QUANTITY

FIELD OBSERVATIONS

DATE:	TIME:

LOCATION / HABITAT:

SEASON:	WEATHER:

BIRD NAME:

BIRD NAME:

SCIENTIFIC NAME:

OF BIRDS SPOTTED: 1   2   3   4   5   6   7   8   9   10   11+

SIGHTS:

SOUNDS:

APPEARANCE:

OBSERVATIONS:

ACTIVITY:

FIELD OBSERVATIONS

IMPRESSIONS:

EQUIPMENT / FURNISHINGS:

RECOMMENDED GUIDE BOOK(S):

RECOMMENDED MAPS(S):

DRIVING/HIKING DIRECTIONS:

PHOTO

IMAGE FILE NAME:

CAMERA EQUIPMENT:

SKETCH

MARKINGS/FEATURES:

BIRD SIGHTINGS SPECIES	HABITAT	QUANTITY

BIRD SIGHTINGS SPECIES	HABITAT	QUANTITY

FIELD OBSERVATIONS

DATE:

TIME:

LOCATION / HABITAT:

SEASON:

WEATHER:

BIRD NAME:

BIRD NAME:

SCIENTIFIC NAME:

OF BIRDS SPOTTED: 1   2   3   4   5   6   7   8   9   10   11+

SIGHTS:

SOUNDS:

APPEARANCE:

OBSERVATIONS:

ACTIVITY:

FIELD OBSERVATIONS

IMPRESSIONS:

EQUIPMENT / FURNISHINGS:

RECOMMENDED GUIDE BOOK(S):

RECOMMENDED MAPS(S):

DRIVING/HIKING DIRECTIONS:

PHOTO

IMAGE FILE NAME:

CAMERA EQUIPMENT:

SKETCH

MARKINGS/FEATURES:

BIRD SIGHTINGS SPECIES	HABITAT	QUANTITY

BIRD SIGHTINGS SPECIES	HABITAT	QUANTITY

FIELD OBSERVATIONS

DATE:	TIME:

LOCATION / HABITAT:

SEASON:	WEATHER:

BIRD NAME:

BIRD NAME:

SCIENTIFIC NAME:

OF BIRDS SPOTTED: 1   2   3   4   5   6   7   8   9   10   11+

SIGHTS:

SOUNDS:

APPEARANCE:

OBSERVATIONS:

ACTIVITY:

FIELD OBSERVATIONS

IMPRESSIONS:

EQUIPMENT / FURNISHINGS:

RECOMMENDED GUIDE BOOK(S):

RECOMMENDED MAPS(S):

DRIVING/HIKING DIRECTIONS:

PHOTO

IMAGE FILE NAME:

CAMERA EQUIPMENT:

SKETCH

MARKINGS/FEATURES:

BIRD SIGHTINGS SPECIES	HABITAT	QUANTITY

BIRD SIGHTINGS SPECIES	HABITAT	QUANTITY

FIELD OBSERVATIONS

DATE:

TIME:

LOCATION / HABITAT:

SEASON:

WEATHER:

BIRD NAME:

BIRD NAME:

SCIENTIFIC NAME:

OF BIRDS SPOTTED: 1   2   3   4   5   6   7   8   9   10   11+

SIGHTS:

SOUNDS:

APPEARANCE:

OBSERVATIONS:

ACTIVITY:

FIELD OBSERVATIONS

IMPRESSIONS:

EQUIPMENT / FURNISHINGS:

RECOMMENDED GUIDE BOOK(S):

RECOMMENDED MAPS(S):

DRIVING/HIKING DIRECTIONS:

PHOTO

IMAGE FILE NAME:

CAMERA EQUIPMENT:

SKETCH

MARKINGS/FEATURES:

BIRD SIGHTINGS SPECIES	HABITAT	QUANTITY

BIRD SIGHTINGS SPECIES	HABITAT	QUANTITY

FIELD OBSERVATIONS

DATE:

TIME:

LOCATION / HABITAT:

SEASON:

WEATHER:

BIRD NAME:

BIRD NAME:

SCIENTIFIC NAME:

OF BIRDS SPOTTED: 1   2   3   4   5   6   7   8   9   10   11+

SIGHTS:

SOUNDS:

APPEARANCE:

OBSERVATIONS:

ACTIVITY:

FIELD OBSERVATIONS

IMPRESSIONS:

EQUIPMENT / FURNISHINGS:

RECOMMENDED GUIDE BOOK(S):

RECOMMENDED MAPS(S):

DRIVING/HIKING DIRECTIONS:

PHOTO

IMAGE FILE NAME:

CAMERA EQUIPMENT:

SKETCH

MARKINGS/FEATURES:

BIRD SIGHTINGS SPECIES	HABITAT	QUANTITY

BIRD SIGHTINGS SPECIES	HABITAT	QUANTITY

FIELD OBSERVATIONS

DATE:

TIME:

LOCATION / HABITAT:

SEASON:

WEATHER:

BIRD NAME:

BIRD NAME:

SCIENTIFIC NAME:

OF BIRDS SPOTTED: 1   2   3   4   5   6   7   8   9   10   11+

SIGHTS:

SOUNDS:

APPEARANCE:

OBSERVATIONS:

ACTIVITY:

FIELD OBSERVATIONS

IMPRESSIONS:

EQUIPMENT / FURNISHINGS:

RECOMMENDED GUIDE BOOK(S):

RECOMMENDED MAPS(S):

DRIVING/HIKING DIRECTIONS:

PHOTO

IMAGE FILE NAME:

CAMERA EQUIPMENT:

SKETCH

MARKINGS/FEATURES:

BIRD SIGHTINGS SPECIES	HABITAT	QUANTITY

BIRD SIGHTINGS SPECIES	HABITAT	QUANTITY

FIELD OBSERVATIONS

DATE:

TIME:

LOCATION / HABITAT:

SEASON:

WEATHER:

BIRD NAME:

BIRD NAME:

SCIENTIFIC NAME:

OF BIRDS SPOTTED: 1   2   3   4   5   6   7   8   9   10   11+

SIGHTS:

SOUNDS:

APPEARANCE:

OBSERVATIONS:

ACTIVITY:

FIELD OBSERVATIONS

IMPRESSIONS:

EQUIPMENT / FURNISHINGS:

RECOMMENDED GUIDE BOOK(S):

RECOMMENDED MAPS(S):

DRIVING/HIKING DIRECTIONS:

PHOTO

IMAGE FILE NAME:

CAMERA EQUIPMENT:

SKETCH

MARKINGS/FEATURES:

BIRD SIGHTINGS SPECIES	HABITAT	QUANTITY

BIRD SIGHTINGS SPECIES	HABITAT	QUANTITY

FIELD OBSERVATIONS

DATE:	TIME:

LOCATION / HABITAT:

SEASON:	WEATHER:

BIRD NAME:

BIRD NAME:

SCIENTIFIC NAME:

OF BIRDS SPOTTED: 1   2   3   4   5   6   7   8   9   10   11+

SIGHTS:

SOUNDS:

APPEARANCE:

OBSERVATIONS:

ACTIVITY:

FIELD OBSERVATIONS

IMPRESSIONS:

EQUIPMENT / FURNISHINGS:

RECOMMENDED GUIDE BOOK(S):

RECOMMENDED MAPS(S):

DRIVING/HIKING DIRECTIONS:

PHOTO

IMAGE FILE NAME:

CAMERA EQUIPMENT:

SKETCH

MARKINGS/FEATURES:

BIRD SIGHTINGS SPECIES	HABITAT	QUANTITY

BIRD SIGHTINGS SPECIES	HABITAT	QUANTITY

FIELD OBSERVATIONS

DATE:

TIME:

LOCATION / HABITAT:

SEASON:

WEATHER:

BIRD NAME:

BIRD NAME:

SCIENTIFIC NAME:

OF BIRDS SPOTTED: 1   2   3   4   5   6   7   8   9   10   11+

SIGHTS:

SOUNDS:

APPEARANCE:

OBSERVATIONS:

ACTIVITY:

FIELD OBSERVATIONS

IMPRESSIONS:

EQUIPMENT / FURNISHINGS:

RECOMMENDED GUIDE BOOK(S):

RECOMMENDED MAPS(S):

DRIVING/HIKING DIRECTIONS:

PHOTO

IMAGE FILE NAME:

CAMERA EQUIPMENT:

SKETCH

MARKINGS/FEATURES:

BIRD SIGHTINGS SPECIES	HABITAT	QUANTITY

BIRD SIGHTINGS SPECIES	HABITAT	QUANTITY

FIELD OBSERVATIONS

DATE:	TIME:

LOCATION / HABITAT:

SEASON:	WEATHER:

BIRD NAME:

BIRD NAME:

SCIENTIFIC NAME:

OF BIRDS SPOTTED: 1   2   3   4   5   6   7   8   9   10   11+

SIGHTS:

SOUNDS:

APPEARANCE:

OBSERVATIONS:

ACTIVITY:

FIELD OBSERVATIONS

IMPRESSIONS:

EQUIPMENT / FURNISHINGS:

RECOMMENDED GUIDE BOOK(S):

RECOMMENDED MAPS(S):

DRIVING/HIKING DIRECTIONS:

PHOTO

IMAGE FILE NAME:

CAMERA EQUIPMENT:

SKETCH

MARKINGS/FEATURES:

BIRD SIGHTINGS SPECIES	HABITAT	QUANTITY

Printed in Great Britain
by Amazon